11/15

D0943690

# eXTREME AIRCRAFT

## IAN F. MAHANEY

**PowerKiDS press**

New York

West Chester Public Library
415 N Church Street
West Chester, PA 19380

Published in 2016 by
**The Rosen Publishing Group, Inc.**
29 East 21st Street, New York, NY 10010

Copyright © 2016 by The Rosen Publishing Group, Inc.

All rights reserved. No part of this book may be reproduced in any form
without permission in writing from the publisher, except by a reviewer.

Developed and produced for Rosen by BlueAppleWorks Inc.

Art Director: T. J. Choleva
Managing Editor for BlueAppleWorks: Melissa McClellan
Designer:  Joshua Avramson
Photo Research: Jane Reid
Editor: Janice Dyer

Photo Credits:
Cover U.S. Air Force photo/Master Sgt. Val Gempis/Public Domain; cover bottom U.S. Air Force photo/Master Sgt. Kevin Gruenwald/Public Domain; title page U.S. Navy photo/Photographer's Mate 2nd Class Saul McSween/Public Domain; p. 4–5 IM_photo/Shutterstock; p. 4 Photographer's Mate 2nd Class Saul McSween, US Navy/Public Domain; p. 5 VanderWolf Images/Shutterstock; p. 6–7 OPIS Zagreb/Shutterstock; p. 6 top left Library of Congress Prints and Photographs Division/Public Domain; p. 6 bottom left Ralf Manteufel/Creative Commons; p. 7 top Casey Deshong/Public Domain; p. 8, 8–9, 9 Frederic Legrand-COMEO/Shutterstock; p. 10–11 Paul Drabot/Shutterstock; p. 10 bottom DearEdward/Creative Commons; p. 10 right Andy Mitchell/Creative Commons; p. 11 top Gordon Tipene/Dreamstime; p. 12–13 William87/Dreamstime; p. 12 left Nadezhda1906/Dreamstime; p. 13 top BriYYZ/Creative Commons; p. 14 left Bureau of Land Management/Creative Commons; p. 14–15 Spc. Matthew Burnett, 115th Mobile Public Affairs Detachment, Oregon National Guard/Public Domain; p. 15 right Alan Wilson/Creative Commons; p. 16 top Heather Nicaise/Dreamstime; p. 16 middle Flaviano Fabrizi/Dreamstime; p.16 bottom Richair/Dreamstime; p. 16–17 Molli66/Dreamstime; p. 17 top tankist276/Shutterstock; p. 18 left U.S. Navy photo/Mass Communication Specialist 2nd Class Patrick W. Mullen III/Public Domain; p. 18 right U.S. Air Force photo/1st Lt. Neil Senkowski/Public Domain; p. 18–19 U.S. Air Force photo/Tech Sgt Keith Brown/Public Domain; p. 19 top U.S. Navy photographer Mass Communication Specialist 1st Class Carmichael Yepez/Public Domain; p. 19 right U.S. Air Force photo/Scott H. Spitzer/Public Domain; p. 20 Michael Pereckas/Creative Commons; p. 20–21 U.S. Air Force photo/Master Sgt. John R. Nimmo/Public Domain; p. 21 right United States Marine Corps photo/Lance Cpl. Neysa Huertas Quinone/Public Domain; p. 22 U.S. Air Force photo/Tech. Sgt. Roy A. Santana/Public Domain; p. 22–23, 23 U.S. Air Force photo/Public Domain; p. 24 left USAF/Brian Shul/Public Domain; p. 24 right The Central Intelligence Agency/Public Domain; p. 24–25 Judson Brohmer/USAF/Public Domain; p. 25 right Ken Hackman, U.S. Air Force photo/Ken Hackman/Public Domain; p. 26 left U.S. Navy photo/Mass Communication Specialist 2nd Class Jason R. Zalasky/Public Domain; p. 26 right DoD photo/Senior Airman Laura Yahemiak, U.S. Air Force/Public Domain; p. 27 United States Marine Corps/ Cpl. Theodore Ritchie/Public Domain; p. 28 WPPilot/Creative Commons; p. 29 NASA/Public Domain; p. 29 top Patrick Beck/Public Domain.

**Cataloging-in-Publication-Data**
Mahaney, Ian F.
Extreme aircraft / by Ian F. Mahaney.
p. cm. — (Extreme machines)
Includes index.
ISBN 978-1-4994-1183-6 (pbk.)
ISBN 978-1-4994-1211-6 (6 pack)
ISBN 978-1-4994-1208-6 (library binding)
1. Airplanes — Juvenile literature. I. Mahaney, Ian F. II. Title.
TL547.M3484 2016
629.133'34—d23

Manufactured in the United States of America
CPSIA Compliance Information: Batch #WS15PK: For Further Information contact: Rosen Publishing, New York, New York at 1-800-237-9932

# Contents

# What Are Aircraft?

Aircraft are machines that fly, like airplanes and helicopters. Airplanes fly by moving fast so air flows over and under their wings. The wings are shaped so that air moves faster over the top of the wings than below the wings. The air pressure above the wings is lower than the air pressure below the wings. This difference in air pressure lifts the wings of an airplane into the air. The shape of the wings is called an **airfoil**.

Aircraft transport passengers and freight. Some aircraft help the military. They carry troops or cargo. Some military aircraft are armed with guns or bombs.

Pilots sit in the part of the airplane called a cockpit. Cockpits contain many control panels and displays that pilots use to fly the plane.

## Powerful Machines

Helicopters have airfoils, but they are shaped differently than an airplane's airfoils. Helicopters have rotors. This is a group of two or more airfoils that spin. The shape of the rotor blades allows the helicopter to **ascend** in the air.

Most aircraft are designed to land on the ground. Other aircraft land on water. Still other aircraft can land in both places. Extreme aircraft are the airplanes and helicopters that do extreme work.

The military uses powerful aircraft to transport troops or cargo. These aircraft are armed with weapons.

Airplanes use jet engines to travel quickly through the air.

Orville and Wilbur Wright flew the world's first airplane in 1903. The plane was called the Wright Flyer and it weighed 605 pounds (275 kg). The Wright Flyer was 21 feet (6.4 m) long and its wingspan measured 40 feet (12.2 m). A plane's wingspan is the distance from the tip of one wing to the tip of the other wing.

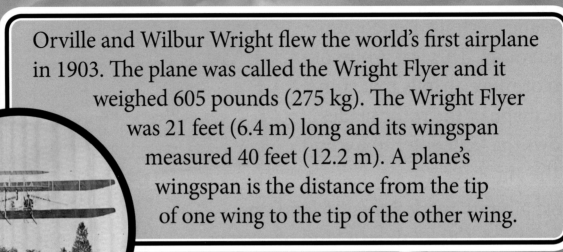

The Antonov An-225 has 32 wheels to help it land safely with large loads.

The Antonov An-225 has the world record for carrying the heaviest payload. It is also the longest and heaviest airplane ever built.

## Mighty Giant

Airplanes can be much bigger today. The biggest plane ever built was made in the **Soviet Union**. The Antonov An-225 is a jet built in the 1980s. Its powerful jet engines pull air through the engine to burn fuel. The Antonov An-225 has 6 engines and is 275 feet (84 m) long. Its wingspan is 290 feet (88 m) wide.

The Soviet Union built only one Antonov An-225 and it carries freight. The payload of the Antonov An-225 is more than 500,000 pounds (227,000 kg). A plane's payload is the amount of weight the airplane can carry in the air. The Antonov An-225 can carry a space shuttle on its roof. It can also fit train cars or tanks in its cargo hold.

# Extreme Solar-Powered Flight

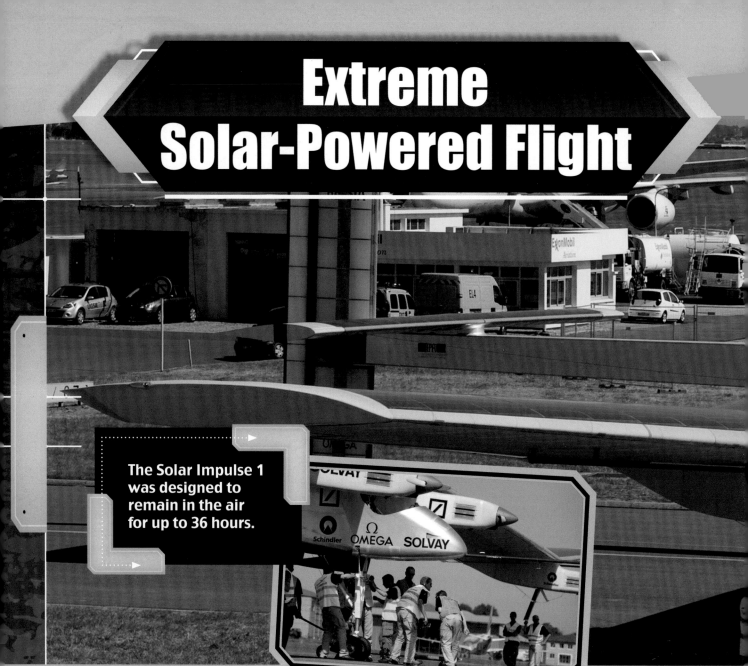

The Solar Impulse 1 was designed to remain in the air for up to 36 hours.

Most aircraft burn fuel. This fuel powers the engine so the aircraft can fly. Other airplanes are powered by electricity. Some of these planes carry batteries that power flight. Other planes make electricity on board using **solar energy**.

The Solar Impulse planes are extreme examples of electrical planes. They rely on solar energy to fly during the day. These planes also store solar energy in batteries so they can fly at night. The Solar Impulse planes are the first electrical planes that can fly at any time of the day.

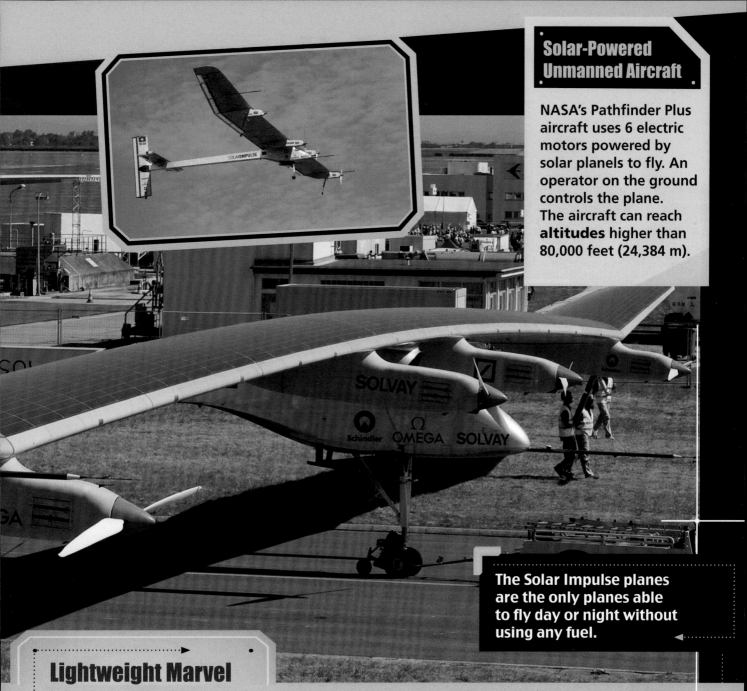

### Solar-Powered Unmanned Aircraft

NASA's Pathfinder Plus aircraft uses 6 electric motors powered by solar planels to fly. An operator on the ground controls the plane. The aircraft can reach **altitudes** higher than 80,000 feet (24,384 m).

The Solar Impulse planes are the only planes able to fly day or night without using any fuel.

## Lightweight Marvel

The Solar Impulse project began in 2003. In 2012, Solar Impulse 1 flew from Spain to Switzerland. Then it flew 19 hours overnight to Morocco. Solar Impulse 1 also flew across the United States. The Solar Impulse 1 is huge, but lightweight. Its wingspan is 208 feet (63.5 m), but it weighs 3,520 pounds (1,600 kg). That's about the same as a car. The Solar Impulse 2 is slightly larger. Its wingspan is 236 feet (72 m) but it only holds one pilot. The Solar Impulse project team is trying to make Solar Impulse 2 the first electric plane to fly around the world!

# Extreme Airliners

## Airbus A380

Today's passenger airplanes are huge. The biggest passenger airplane in the world is the Airbus A380. The wingspan is 262 feet (80 m) and it is 239 feet (73 m) long. The A380 is a double-decker plane that normally seats 525 passengers. The Airbus 380 can carry more than 800 passengers if the arrangement of seats is changed. Most of these planes have showers and lounges for some of the passengers.

Because the upper deck is so far away from the engines, the Airbus A380 is very quiet for passengers.

The Airbus A380 is powered by 4 jet engines and can fly nonstop from Dallas, Texas, to Sydney, Australia. Its cruising speed is 560 miles (900 km) per hour.

## Did You Know?

The Boeing 747-8 is another huge double-decker passenger airliner. It is the largest aircraft built in the United States. It can carry 467 passengers.

The Airbus A380 is so big that it can only land at airports with special facilities that can handle it.

## Cruising in Style

Huge passenger planes like the A380 can fly long distances. They can cross continents and take passengers over oceans. The A380 can fly 9,700 miles (15,600 km) without refueling and its cruising speed is 560 miles (900 km) per hour. A plane's cruising speed is a speed that is fast but also burns fuel **efficiently**.

# Boeing 777s

Boeing makes several aircraft with the model numbers 777 and 777X. They have a nickname, the "triple 7s." These passenger aircraft can fly the furthest in the world. One of Boeing's passenger models, the 777-200LR, can fly more than 10,000 miles (16,100 km) without refueling. This distance is called the plane's range. The 777-200LR also carries about 300 passengers.

The 777-200ER can carry between 300 and 400 passengers. The 777-200ER, like other 777s and big airplanes, is known as a wide bodied aircraft. This means the passenger plane has two aisles that divide the seats. A narrow bodied aircraft has one aisle and carries fewer passengers.

The triple 7s have 6 wheels on each main landing gear. It takes about 49 days to build one of these huge aircraft.

## Flying Far

Boeing's 777-8X can carry 350 passengers on a trip almost as far as a 777-200LR. The 777-8X, like the 777-9X, offers improved fuel efficiency, too.

Boeing also makes 777 freighters. These aircraft have two decks for cargo. Instead of carrying passengers on the main deck, Boeing uses the main deck for freight. All 777s and 777Xs also have space on the lower deck for cargo. The total payload for 777 freighters is 224,000 pounds (102,000 kg).

### Did You Know?

Boeing's 777-330 holds the most passengers of all the 777 aircraft. It an carry up to 550 passengers.

Cargo companies like FedEx use the 777s to carry packages around the world.

# Extreme Jobs

## Fighting Forest Fires

Forest fires burn millions of **acres** of trees and brush in the United States every year. These fires also threaten houses and other buildings.

Aircraft help the U.S. Forest Service and its firefighters battle these fires. The Forest Service uses helicopters to transport firefighters and cargo so the firefighters can fight fires. Helicopters can also drop water or fire retardant on blazes. Fire retardants are chemicals that stop or slow a spreading fire. One of the largest fire-fighting helicopters is the Boeing 234 Chinook helicopter. The U.S. Army first used Chinook helicopters to transport troops and cargo. The **civilian** version of the Chinook can drop 3,000 gallons (11,350 l) of water or fire retardant to help fight a fire.

Helicopters can also be used to fight forest fires. They drop water from their tanks onto the burning trees.

This Douglas DC-7 is dropping fire retardant on a wildfire in Oregon.

The Evergreen Supertanker is a modified Boeing 747 used to fight fires in California. It can carry 24,000 gallons (90,850 l) of water or fire retardant.

## Fire-Fighting Jets

The Forest Service and other fire-fighting agencies also use planes for much of their fire-fighting strategy. Jumbo jets are wide bodied aircraft that were originally made to carry passengers and freight. Jumbo jets like the McDonnell Douglas DC10 can also fight fires. This passenger plane was modified to carry 12,000 gallons (45,425 l) of water or fire retardant in a tank. The jet then drops the water or fire retardant on the fire.

# Across Water and Land

Amphibious aircraft help in search and rescue operations. Amphibious airplanes help fight forest fires, too. The Bombardier 415 can fly over the surface of a lake, scoop 1,600 gallons (6,000 l) of water into a tank, and drop the water on a fire. The 415 can then release its wheels and land on the ground.

The Bombardier 415 Superscooper is an amphibious aircraft built in Canada. It was built specifically to quickly deliver huge amounts of water to fires.

## Multitasking Seaplanes

All planes and helicopters have landing gear. This allows them to return safely to Earth. Most planes have wheels so they can land on the ground. Seaplanes have landing gear that allows them to land on and take off from water. There are two types of seaplanes. Floatplanes have **pontoons** instead of wheels. Flying boats have hulls that float. Both types of seaplanes can be amphibious. This means they can land on ground and in water. Amphibious planes have wheels for landing on hard surfaces like airport runways. The wheels retract when the plane is on water.

Seaplanes are sometimes used to drop water on forest fires. They also carry passengers to remote areas surrounded by water.

# Military Super Flyers

## The Globemaster

Military forces around the world use aircraft to protect the skies around their countries. Some aircraft gather **intelligence** and other aircraft carry guns or bombs. Still other military aircraft transport cargo and troops.

The United States uses a plane, the Boeing C-17 Globemaster III, to transport troops and cargo around the world. The Globemaster's payload is 164,000 pounds (74,500 kg). It can carry an M-1 tank or two rows of army trucks.

The Globemaster has 54 permanent seats for passengers. It can also seat 128 more passengers instead of cargo. Two pilots control the plane and two passengers can fly in the cockpit.

The Boeing C-17 Globemaster III is also used to evacuate people in medical emergencies and to drop supplies for troops on the ground.

The Boeing C-17 Globemaster can land in small airfields and on harsh terrain anywhere in the world, day or night.

The Lockheed Martin C-5 Galaxy can transport more cargo than any other aircraft. It can carry tanks or up to 5 helicopters.

## Midair Fill

The Globemaster can fly 2,400 nautical miles without refueling. A nautical mile is a unit of measure used for sea and air travel. A nautical mile equals 1.15 miles (1.85 km) and is used to take into account the Earth's shape. The Globemaster can refuel in the air. The Air Force KC 135 Stratotanker refuels planes in midair. The Globemaster flies under and slightly behind the KC 135. An operator on the Stratotanker then **maneuvers** a boom into the Globemaster's fuel tank. A boom includes the tanker's hose and nozzle. Fuel is then pumped from the KC 135 through the boom to the Globemaster.

# Invisible Fighters

Radar is a system that helps users find objects that they cannot see. To determine what objects are nearby, a radar operator sends a signal from a radar **transmitter**. When the signal reaches an object, it bounces back to the transmitter. The radar operator can figure out the size, speed, and direction of the object.

Military forces around the world use radar to find out where aircraft are located. Most planes try to hide from enemies' radar. Beginning in the 1950s, the United States' U-2 spy planes flew at high altitudes to hide from radar. These planes could fly 70,000 feet (21,300 m) in the air. This is twice the height of commercial airliners.

The U-2 is nicknamed "Dragon Lady." The pilot of the U-2 wears a type of space suit to ensure a steady supply of oxygen.

## Did You Know?

The F-117A Nighthawk is the first **stealth** aircraft flown by the United States.

The Lockheed Martin F-35 Lightning II aircraft is designed to avoid radar and travel at supersonic speed.

## Extreme Speed

During the 1970s, the U.S. Armed Forces began developing planes that could hide from radar. These planes are called stealth aircraft. Stealth aircraft try to move in secret so enemy radar can't see them. The Armed Forces worked with plane manufacturer Lockheed Martin on the F-35 Lightning II in the 1990s. The F-35 is a stealth aircraft that hides from radar and can fly at 1,200 miles (1,900 km) per hour.

# Stealth Bombers

Toward the end of **World War II**, German Armed Forces finished building the first stealth aircraft. It never entered combat. The aircraft was covered in charcoal dust and wood glue. The Germans thought these materials would absorb the signals from enemy radar. Planes are normally made of metal and radar can see metal objects very well. The German scientists thought that by coating metal in other substances they could hide their aircraft from radar.

The U.S. military and its contractors used similar technologies when developing stealth aircraft. The Northrop Grumman B-2 Spirit Stealth Bomber is made from graphite. Graphite is a material that absorbs radar. The B-2 Spirit is flatter than other aircraft. Radar operators have trouble seeing the plane because signals bounce off the plane rather than returning to the transmitter.

The B-2 Spirit has a crew of two, a pilot and a mission commander. The aircraft was designed to travel deep into enemy territory without being seen.

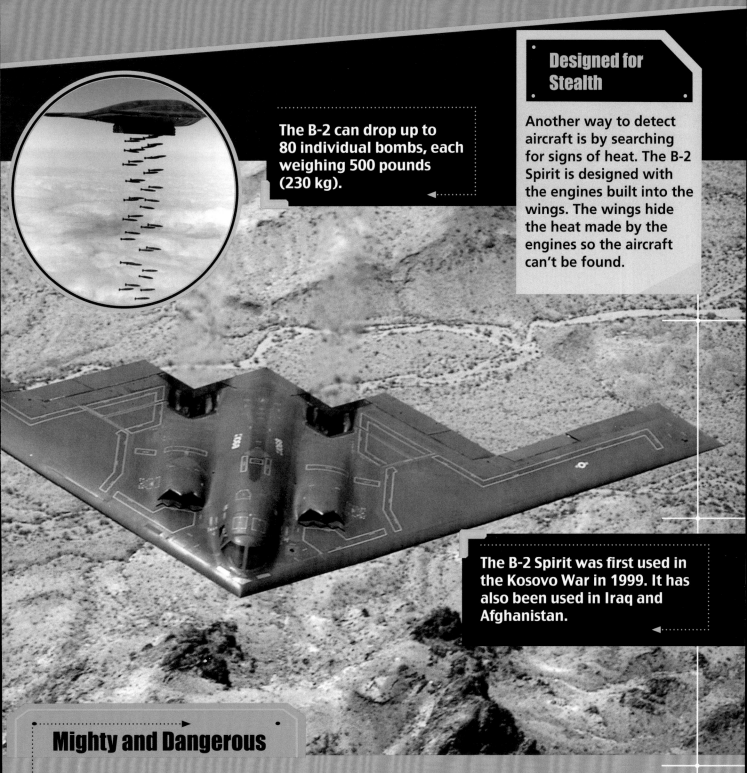

The B-2 can drop up to 80 individual bombs, each weighing 500 pounds (230 kg).

## Designed for Stealth

Another way to detect aircraft is by searching for signs of heat. The B-2 Spirit is designed with the engines built into the wings. The wings hide the heat made by the engines so the aircraft can't be found.

The B-2 Spirit was first used in the Kosovo War in 1999. It has also been used in Iraq and Afghanistan.

## Mighty and Dangerous

The B-2 Spirit has a payload of 40,000 pounds (18,000 kg). That's enough to carry a nuclear warhead. The plane can also climb to 50,000 feet (15,200 m) in the air. It can fly 6,000 miles (9,700 km) without refueling. When it needs fuel, a KC-135 Stratotanker can deliver fuel to the B-2 Spirit. Then the bomber can fly another 4,000 miles (6,400 km) before it needs more fuel.

# The World's Fastest Flyer

In 1960, the Soviet Union shot down a United States U-2 spy plane. The U-2 aircraft was flying at 70,000 feet (21,300 m). The U-2 incident made the Air Force use spy planes that could fly even higher. The Blackbird SR-71 could fly at 85,000 feet (25,900 m) and is also the fastest manned air-breathing aircraft ever made. An air-breathing aircraft has an engine that burns fuel by combining the fuel with oxygen from the air.

The Blackbird SR-71 could fly faster than the speed of sound. Just like an aircraft or a bird, it takes time for sound to travel through the air. The speed of sound is Mach 1 or about 760 miles (1,225 km) per hour at sea level. The speed of sounds slows at higher altitudes. Jets that fly faster than Mach 1 are called supersonic.

The SR-71 was designed to fly with two pilots at speeds of Mach 3.

## Did You Know?

The Blackbird SR-71 set the speed record in 1976. The speed was 2,193 miles (3,530 km) per hour.

Specialized KC-135 tankers were used to refuel the SR-71 in midair and at high speeds.

## Retired with Honor

Blackbird SR-71s were made of titanium. Titanium is a strong metal that can withstand high heat. Blackbirds' engines could get as hot as 800 degrees Fahrenheit (427 degrees C). Blackbird SR-71s were also stealth aircraft. They were covered in iron paint because that helps absorb radar. After 26 years of service, the Air Force retired the Blackbird SR-71 planes in 1990.

# Extreme Powered Lift

Helicopters can hover. This means they can stay suspended in midair. They move only slightly back and forth or up and down. Most airplanes can't hover. Airplanes need to move fast to stay in the air. Helicopters can land in a smaller space than airplanes, but airplanes are much faster than helicopters. Troops on airplanes can travel quickly to missions, but troops on helicopters can land in places that airplanes can't land.

The U.S. Department of Defense worked with two companies, Boeing and Bell Helicopters, to develop an extreme aircraft. The Osprey V-22 can lift from the ground like a helicopter, then fly like an airplane. The Osprey is a tiltrotor aircraft. This means its rotors can sit upright on its wings to ascend like a helicopter. The rotors can also rotate to act as airplane propellers.

The Osprey V-22 can hover and land like a helicopter, and fly long distances at high speeds like an airplane.

## Troop Carriers

Osprey V-22s go on many missions. The aircraft can make vertical takeoffs and landings (VTOL). They can also make short takeoffs and landings (STOL). Ospreys can carry 24 troops for 390 miles (630 km). They can also carry up to 20,000 pounds (9,100 kg) of cargo.

**Did You Know?**

The Osprey V-22 can fly at speeds of 400 miles (645 km) per hour. This is twice as fast as a helicopter.

The V-22 entered service with the U.S. Marine Corps in 2007 and the Air Force in 2009. Since then, it has been used in combat and rescue missions in Iraq, Afghanistan, Sudan, and Libya.

# Space Planes

Rockets are different from jets. Rockets store oxygen and do not require outside oxygen like the Blackbird SR-71 does. Rockets are faster than jets. Rockets propelled the U.S. space shuttles into space at more than 17,000 miles (27,350 km) per hour. This is called hypersonic speed. It is more than 5 times the speed of sound. Space shuttles and their rockets took astronauts into space for research. In 1990, the Space Shuttle *Discovery* launched the Hubble Telescope into orbit. The Hubble Telescope takes pictures of outer space.

Many governments worldwide plan to make space planes. Private companies want to take tourists into space, too. It will take extreme aircraft to get there. Space planes of the future may be similar to the U.S. space shuttles. Rockets may need to power the space planes.

The SpaceShipOne is an example of a space plane. This type of vehicle acts as an aircraft while on Earth and a spacecraft while in space.

The Buran spacecraft was the first space shuttle to perform an unmanned flight. This Soviet-made spacecraft made its only flight in 1988.

## Spacecraft to the Moon

*Apollo 11* was the first spacecraft to land humans on the moon. Americans Neil Armstrong and Buzz Aldrin were the first to walk on the moon in 1969.

The Space Shuttle *Discovery* was launched and landed 39 times over 27 years. It made more spaceflights than any other spacecraft. The *Discovery* is retired and is on display at the Smithsonian Museum.

## Into the Future

Extreme aircraft have helped humans fly to amazing parts of the world and accomplish incredible things. In the future, extreme aircraft may take people to outer space. Those extreme aircraft may be rockets. They may also be jets that take off from a runway on Earth, fly into space, and return to the same runway.

# GLOSSARY

**acres**  Units of measure. One acre equals 43,560 square feet (4,047 sq m).

**airfoil**  The shape of an airplane wing or helicopter rotor that lifts the aircraft in the air.

**altitudes**  Heights above Earth's surface.

**ascend**  To move upward.

**civilian**  Not belonging to the military.

**efficiently**  Done in the quickest, best way possible.

**intelligence**  Information gathered about a person or country, usually for a government.

**maneuver**  To move easily.

**pontoons**  Long floats that look like skis.

**solar energy**  Energy from the sun.

**Soviet Union**  A former country that stretched from eastern Europe across Asia to the Pacific Ocean.

**stealth**  Secret, sneaky movement.

**transmitter**  A machine that sends out a signal.

**World War II**  A war fought by the United States, Great Britain, France, and the Soviet Union against Germany, Japan, and Italy from 1939 to 1945.

## Further Reading

Dos Santos, Julie. *Aircraft.*
New York, NY: Cavendish Square Publishing, 2009.

Hammelef, Danielle S. *Building an Airplane.*
North Mankato, MN: Capstone Press, 2014.

Nahum, Andrew. *Flight.*
New York, NY: DK Eyewitness Books, 2011.

Portman, Michael. *Fighter Jets.*
New York, NY: Gareth Stevens Publishing, 2013.

Shank, Carol. *U.S. Military Assault Vehicles.*
North Mankato, MN: Capstone Press, 2012.

Sutton, Felix. *We Were There at the First Airplane Flight.*
Mineola, NY: Dover Publications, Reprint edition 2013.

## Websites

Due to the changing nature of Internet links, PowerKids Press has developed an online list of websites related to the subject of this book. This site is updated regularly. Please use this link to access the list:
**www.powerkidslinks.com/em/air**

# INDEX